LIVING CHAOS

SNEHA VIKASH

Copyright © Sneha Vikash
All Rights Reserved.

ISBN 978-1-64983-060-9

This book has been published with all efforts taken to make the material error-free after the consent of the author. However, the author and the publisher do not assume and hereby disclaim any liability to any party for any loss, damage, or disruption caused by errors or omissions, whether such errors or omissions result from negligence, accident, or any other cause.

While every effort has been made to avoid any mistake or omission, this publication is being sold on the condition and understanding that neither the author nor the publishers or printers would be liable in any manner to any person by reason of any mistake or omission in this publication or for any action taken or omitted to be taken or advice rendered or accepted on the basis of this work. For any defect in printing or binding the publishers will be liable only to replace the defective copy by another copy of this work then available.

Contents

Preface .... *ix*

1. Little Chaos 1
2. Scarred 2
3. Storms 3
4. Silence 4
5. Dark 5
6. Vulnerability 6
7. Norms 7
8. Contradictions 9
9. Bare Skin 10
10. Restless 11
11. Mirror 12
12. Speak Out 14
13. Backspace 16
14. Body 18
15. Space 20
16. Rememory 22
17. Carefree 23
18. Battles 25
19. Fear 26
20. Shades 28
21. Blooded Hands 29
22. Canvas 31
23. A Character 32

Contents

24. Lies	34
25. Rainbow	36
26. Wings	37
27. Sadness	38
28. Smile	39
29. Sunset	40
30. Darkness	41
31. A Part-time Writer	43

"to the chaotic hearts and minds"

"Every chaotic mind, evolves great Art"

Preface

This book would take you to a pool of emotions, it will make you see the light that makes itself felt only when darkness prevails. Every page that you turn will be a rollercoaster where you might find yourself engulfed by the darkness and chaos but as Life goes on, this book too shall continue to take you to its end.

LET'S LIVE THE CHAOS.

1. Little Chaos

There's a little chaos in everything,
Some, I dress as a knight robe,
Others, I adorn in my mind.
Every chaos outshines you.

2. Scarred

I'm more of a scarred story,
With thorns pricking the skin,
Touched million times,
Not holy, I tell you,
Blooded,
Blooded all over,
The craters of my skin.
Scars breathe to let you know,
Those craters could grow flowers.

3. Storms

I have had enough
Of the Sun and the Moon,
Now, I wish to be a part
Of the Storms,
For, they build me
In ways, no one could
Break me off,
Those cracks on your skin,
Would make way for the light.

4. Silence

Those screams have
So much to say,
Only if you know,
What silence conveys,
I do not dwell in the sunrises,
I drown more in the sea,
And crave for sunsets,
Every sun that sets affirms,
It's okay to fall and rise again.

5. Dark

My eyes would tell you,
I grow more flower in tears,
Weed blooms in my smile,
Yet, it begins and ends
With darkness,
But it is satisfying to be
A monochromic story
Every dark has a story to convey.

6. Vulnerability

I take you across the sea,
But you hide through,
You say that the waves
Are engulfing, frightening,
I assure you,
That they aren't,
But you rush back,
To the sea-shore,
I ask you,
What makes it
So scary?
After little silence,
You say,
Their vulnerability.

7. Norms

Too many eyes
On me today,
My shirt crumpled,
Dishearten people's heart,
I do not know,
Who defines it for me,
The norms,
That directs my ways of life,
But how are they ignorant
Of the ways my life
Seems to be crumpled
Under the pressures
To perform well?
Every single moment,
To drive it perfect,
I'm tired today,
With less stamina,
Isn't it fine to be on holiday?
No, not for a day,
Not for a week,
I wish to be on holiday,
That never ends,
For, isn't it fine,

To perform at my own pace,
And just not be in the race?
Isn't it fine,
If I quit to just be, be on my own?
No rules, no comparisons,
Just little struggles,
And my own little slower pace.

8. Contradictions

If you ask the people,
To speak of me,
Some would tell you,
My face shines
In a burst of laughter,
Others,
How most times,
I do not speak a word,
Some would tell you,
I sing songs that echo
In the entire veranda,
Others,
My voice is coarse,
Some may say,
They have
Never seen me cry,
While some cannot even
Handle the outburst,
I have lived different
Parts of me in
Different people,
And you'll surely be
Surprised of the Contradictions.

9. Bare Skin

I have pulled up my skin
Too many times now,
I wish, I could be bare,
Not living in shells
That put me in a box,
I wish to walk out to open fields,
Spread my arms,
Breathe, breathe like,
There's no end, breathe like,
Even if it's the last moment,
I die today, without regrets,
For long, I have been
Saving the world,
Today, I wish to put down
All my arms,
That protects me that helps me
To be the strong,
Today, I wish to be vulnerable,
Today, I wish to be saved.

10. Restless

I'm exhausted my muscles
Don't move anymore,
You want me to put efforts,
It's tiring, I'm restless,
So much chaos,
Words, letters,
So much chaos,
I cannot place them,
Where?
Where do they belong?
I'm forgetting, it's vague,
I cannot see through,
I'm restless,
Nothing is at the place,
It's all chaos,
So much chaos,
Nothing belongs here,
Not even me,
What does?
I don't know,
I told you,
I'm restless.

11. Mirror

With every glance on the mirror
I hate myself a little more,
The ways these curves
Don't find roads to flatness,
The way my hair,
Isn't straight enough,
The way my face seems
Overdone with acne,
Oh, the perfect size,
Oh, the perfect hair,
Oh, the perfect skin,
It just makes me hate myself,
More,
More,
More,
Oh, I damn it tonight,
The perfectness,
The sadness,
The depression,
The anxiety,
But I don't see myself,
Smiling,
All cheerful,

Damn it too,
I wasn't born to be
All happy, no gloom,
I paint myself,
Yet not be ashamed
To just be the monochrome.

12. Speak Out

It's getting darker,
With no voices to talk,
Or people to read,
But none to grasp
The words that need
To be read in between,
Somehow, I tell you,
That I take years
To speak my heart out,
I gather courage
From every corner of
My heart,
Most times,
I'm way too late,
To speak what's meant
To be said,
And people often walk away,
Wanting to hear more,
Yes, I'm talkative,
Yet I do not convey my heart,
Maybe, you should find
Other ways to know,
What I hide,

But I'll tell you,
There are numerous
Secrets untold,
That is still struggling,
To find a way out of me,
To reach where it belongs.

13. Backspace

I could feel myself
Shrinking with the endless load,
That hangs on my wrinkled skin,
Smile now, has been
A distant friend,
"Hey, I miss you,
Can we just catch up real soon?"
My fingers seem desperate to hit
The send button but suddenly
A voice echoes in my head,
Wait!
What if, you are annoying?
Your friend is busy?
Somehow, I'm convinced,
I backspace the letters and
The email resembles me,
Empty, completely empty,
Or maybe curious as water,
Gushing out to meet the sea,
I try to be friends with other faces,
Which are somewhat familiar
But maybe, it always remained
In my shelf as the book,

I never read,
It waves at me but
My hands seem sweaty,
My face pale,
I avoid them, I hate them,
But do I?
It engulfs me
Like a fire in the forest
Who loses all its charm and life,
My voice even trembles now,
Like an impending earthquake
Would gobble up my soul,
But hey, dearest friend,
I hope, you read the letter,
I never wrote.

14. Body

My body is a room
Full of people
And there's an
Endless clatter
That echoes
Making my voice
Unheard, invisible,
I'm looking for a room,
Different than now,
That is serene to my soul
Extremely quiet or a
Balcony that flows
With an endless breeze
In the scorching heat
Even on a starry night sky,
I have rooms,
Other than these
In faces, I have fallen
In love with,
In faces, I have been
Friends with,
I have plenty of them,
There are rooms

With my name written,
But I couldn't knock the doors,
Home, four walls
You say I tell you,
Its emotions, a comma,
Never a full stop,
Houses in different
Directions yet none to stay,
You ask me, why I'm silent,
But how do you I tell you
Of the voices that are
Revolting in my head,
I'm trying to be a fascist
But I'm always overruled
I try to walk streets,
I try to leave home,
But there's not a place,
I could go.

15. Space

I do not occupy space
More than the moon does
On that giant sky,
I own space only to
Make myself feel alive,
I breathe in a room,
They tell me it's not my own,
I'm surprised and I could feel
The stars waving goodbyes,
As if the sky isn't my room anymore,
But why do I have to lose it?
Did I ask for more?
A room of my own,
A room where the breeze
Passes by early morning with
The first rays that fall on my life,
A room of my own,
Where the window panes,
Smile back every other night,
The streets they do not threaten me,
I do not find myself vulnerable to
The world, a room of my own,
Where there's enough

Space to speak of,
Where I do not
Drown in my thoughts,
Where I sail on a stormy night,
I tell you that all I need is
A room of my own,
But you refuse me,
You ask me to be someone else,
How do I live with a mask day & night?
I'm beautiful to be myself,
I'm strong to be myself,
I'm me, all I ask for,
Is a room of my own,
To live, breathe and be.

16. Rememory

I'm often strangled
With a memory; a rememory,
Knocking doors to my soul,
Awakening the dead,
Staying back when it had
Not to stop by me in the first place,
I'm choked with this unfeeling,
My heart seems heavy,
Oh, you rememory,
You saw me again, happiest as ever,
And ruined it, ruined it as ever,
Oh, I cannot remember more,
Maybe you'll come,
No more.

17. Carefree

You remind of the days
Golden as they were,
Just going around the streets,
Carefree, careless,
With no fear in those eyes
Happiness,
Utter happiness that shined,
The curve on that little face
Was real all real, not made up
And the fun stayed,
Always, always,
Even today,
When I do forget
What brought me here?
Was that a smile?
An innocent smile,
I never realized,
How it vanished?
How that beautiful present,
Turned into memories,
That smile turned into the gloom,
I don't know but those smiles are gone,
Those loud tears turned into silence,

Making me feel like a cage,
Yet another race.
Did the twisted reality change?
Or are we all derange?

18. Battles

I know my battles
With depression is endless,
And I, now and then
Find me drowning deep into
The pool of sadness,
My brain hurts always horribly,
And I can't, can't stop the loop of
Thinking overthinking,
Anxiety and pain,
But, I do want it to stop,
Just end go and
Never come back
It's a hopeless dream though,
I try to write more
But words don't find
A place to fit in,
Maybe just how
I don't fit in this world.

19. Fear

I have seen you
Dwelling in the darkness
Steadily and all at once,
You crafted rooms
With dusk and gloom,
Embellishing it with your
Loneliness,
And now,
You fear the Light,
All of us do,
We fear meeting people,
Allowing them spaces
Into our lives,
For we believe more,
Upon the death of love
More than its breathing,
We constantly trust,
The Murk than Bliss,
For bliss we infer,
Doesn't stay,
But can we not,
For once,
Only once,

Reckon upon the
Miracles that light bestows,
And plunge into a vivid world.

20. Shades

These crimson cheeks do not recite,
The solemn songs my mind hums,
These gleaming eyes do not mumble
The sadness that in my heart abides,
I know, I resemble
More to the shades of bliss than
To the monochromes of gloom,
But, but in moments,
These hues fade and glint the paleness,
In moments, all that I shelter, wrecks,
In moments, I fail to brace my
Soul for this body repels,
In moments,
The murk seems deepening,
Hypnotizing me to be its own,
The scars, the bruises, the agony
Pave paths to my mind,
When I await sleep to knock doors,
But this very traitor bids me adieu,
And the web of thoughts seem dense,
And again I resist being a depressing soul
But alas, all the strength goes in vain,
For, this smile still is caged in pain.

21. Blooded Hands

I'm ignorant of
Shaking off these
Constant battles that
Itch to pull me
Closer to you,
But that's not even
A dream now,
You are far, afar,
And this void that
Speaks of you,
That screams for
Your presence
Seems to know
No leaps and bounds,
Maybe, it still hopes
For the little light
That sparks up the darkness
But isn't that an
Elusive miracle now,
A faithless hope,
It's you and me,
At distant parallels,
Not meant to meet,

LIVING CHAOS

But this damned heart
That still longs for you,
I wish it knew,
You weren't home now,
You pushed me out of you,
Into colds and storms,
The hands that were meant
To be the warmth,
Were now the bloodied hands
That slit love into million deaths.

22. Canvas

I dusted off
Characters on a canvas,
With strokes of
Dusk and agony,
Filled with chromes of Hope,
Oh, it turned out
To be poetry of Life
With perfect imperfect
Syllables rhyming,
Not rhyming rhythm,
Colons, semicolons,
Commas and Full stops,
Alluring in its presence.

23. A Character

I died,
When I was born
A character,
From those vacant rooms,
The rocking chair and
The mummed nights, I travelled,
To the world that wasn't mine,
I no more portrayed reality, I lived it,
In the continuous cycle of life,
I broke the pace,
I jumped onto papers and letters,
Inks and signs,
I was slower, more impatient
But happier,
Happier in an illusion
That was born out of me,
I was different,
Lost in those walls,
Built out of nothing concrete,
It was stronger yet,
Out of me, I travelled
Time and space,
To breathe in,

To sleep in
A world that I dreamt,
And to wake up not,
I died tonight,
To live it all over again.

24. Lies

I tell you,
"Life will be okay"
And you ask me,
How often do I lie?
I laugh and say, 'most times',
You roll your eyes,
And I look at you in awe,
Isn't that bad, to lie?
To people who
Look up to you
For the truth?
You ask me,
And I smile, calmly,
Because hurricane
Are meant to storm
In the brain,
Isn't it?
I just try to
Be an umbrella,
Save you from
The damage;
The UV rays,
They harm you,

Just like the truth does,
It pushes you
Into doors that
Are jammed,
That needs repair,
But, I couldn't find a man,
So, I tell you,
It is locked now,
You ask me,
For the keys,
And I lie,
They are lost.

25. Rainbow

It has been easier on some days,
To let the smile be the sunshine,
But other days, it's simply a rainbow
Struggling hard to be felt,
It vanishes with when the
Light seems to find a way out
And reappears when it comes back,
But every rainbow doesn't tell you,
The conflicts it conquers
Between the shades that
Try hard to be vivid,
It doesn't tell you,
How it waits patiently,
For the sun and clouds
To be just friends,
For the thoughts
To just be a clear sky,
For the air to be at ease
And not rush being storms,
Some days, it's too much night,
Other days, it's just plain sunshine.

26. Wings

Those colours
Floating into the Sky,
Reminds me of your flight,
Remember the time,
When you had wings but no fear,
You had happiness but no reasons,
A carefree little world of yours,
That took you to the
Acme of the mountains,
And you didn't know,
How it feels to fall,
Be that, again,
Fear none,
Just be,
Who you are.

27. Sadness

Why do you
Wish to
Dust off
The sadness
You hold?
For,
Sadness
Grinds great
Poetry.

28. Smile

The mirror,
Chants your story,
The story of your valour,
On the murkiest nights,
The scarred dusks,
With minimal sunshine,
That pierced onto your skin,
Yet did not reach your heart,
But, that smile,
The persistent smile,
It makes you the knight,
They fear these eyes,
Full of rage,
They fear the strength
Of those hushed lips,
You speak thunders
Yet smile, smile again,
Tossing and turning,
Those lines onto
Flowery thorns,
They pierce you,
Yet you smile,
Wins you all the shine.

29. Sunset

It has been ages,
I saw the sunset,
I had stayed away
From the things, I loved,
For such a long time,
And now I wish to fall
For them again,
The sky, the clouds and
The sunset and now again,
I want them to find a way
To my poetry.

30. Darkness

Darkness is copiously inspiring,
The way the poem creeps in
With the words falling in places,
The way you remain
Silent yet hold million
Voices within you,
Some that you have
Heard and heard
And has become a noise,
Some that you have
Heard unheard
That has become silence
And if you look within you
You would know,
Darkness never makes
You void,
It fills you, fills you
With all that has
Never found its place
In the world,
So, let it live
Live till it makes
You alive

*And never let it
Go taking away
All that you hold.*

31. A Part-Time Writer

On days,
When the walls of my brain
Restrains from being friends
With news and facts,
I become,
A part-time writer,
Trying to look for blocks
That builds my inner soul,
What repairs the damage
Done by the world?
Poetry is nothing but
A part-time medicine,
That heals wounds that
Eyes fail to see,
On days, when the sun
Seems to not find
It's way out of the clouds,
I become a part-time writer,
Trying to yield the light,
Out of letters that
Brings endurance to each heart
That reads,
On days when the world

Seems to be caught in
The fuss of life,
When hurricanes seem
To find no low tides,
I become a part-time writer,
Trying to pull the thread out
That simplifies the puzzle,
That rules hearts and minds,
On days when you give up,
I quote lines to tell you,
That there's still
A way for you to ride
The sun that you think
Has already been set,
I sow pieces,
On days of wrath,
To calm the youth,
That is being juxtaposed
Between life or survival,
To grow happiness,
That lacks in most eyes,
On days, when you are away,
Walking on paths with no ends,
I become a part-time writer,
To bring you closer to the road
That meets your way.

"Let your chaos that roars within you,

Take you Home."

www.ingramcontent.com/pod-product-compliance
Lightning Source LLC
LaVergne TN
LVHW042002060526
838200LV00041B/1840